Things That Sting

Sea Urchins

By Michael Rajczak

Gareth Stevens
PUBLISHING

Please visit our website, www.garethstevens.com. For a free color catalog of all our high-quality books, call toll free 1-800-542-2595 or fax 1-877-542-2596.

Library of Congress Cataloging-in-Publication Data

Rajczak, Michael, author.
Sea urchins / Michael Rajczak.
pages cm. — (Things that sting)
Includes bibliographical references and index.
ISBN 978-1-4824-1719-7 (pbk.)
ISBN 978-1-4824-1720-3 (6 pack)
ISBN 978-1-4824-1718-0 (library binding)
1. Sea urchins—Juvenile literature. I. Title.
QL384.E2R245 2015
593.9'5—dc23

2014032407

First Edition

Published in 2016 by
Gareth Stevens Publishing
111 East 14th Street, Suite 349
New York, NY 10003

Designer: Nicholas Domiano
Editor: Kristen Rajczak

Photo credits: Cover, p. 1 © iStockphoto.com/ashveen; title texture: Asya Alexandrova/Shutterstock.com; caption box: VectorShots/Shutterstock.com; p. 5 Pelevina Ksinia/Shutterstock.com; p. 7 aquapix/Shutterstock.com; p. 9 Dimitrios/Shutterstock.com; p. 11 noppharat/Shutterstock.com; p. 13 (main) Ken Lucas/Getty Images; p. 13 (inset) Philippe Bourjon/Wikimedia Commons; p. 15 gubgib/Shutterstock.com; p. 17 Jonathan Bird/Getty Images; p. 19 cynoclub/Shutterstock.com; p. 21 (inset) Andrey Nekrasov/Shutterstock.com; p. 21 (main) NatalieJean/Shutterstock.com.

Printed in the United States of America

CPSIA compliance information: Batch #CS16GS: For further information contact Gareth Stevens, New York, New York at 1-800-542-2595.

Contents

Hedgehog of the Sea 4
Urchins Found 6
Body Talk 8
Hanging Around 10
Ouch! 12
Watch Your Step 14
Part of the Web 16
Sea Urchin for Lunch? 18
Amazing Urchins 20
Glossary 22
For More Information 23
Index 24

Words in the glossary appear in **bold** type the first time they are used in the text.

Hedgehog of the Sea

Sea urchins are unusual-looking animals. They're round and covered with many **spines**. Some sea urchins have solid spines. Others have spines that are hollow—and possibly poisonous! These spines are sharp enough to **pierce** the skin of many animals, including people. They **protect** the sea urchin's soft inner body from animals that want to eat it.

The spines aren't the only dangerous parts of the sea urchin. Body parts called pedicellariae (peh-duh-suh-LEHR-ee-uh) can also be **venomous**, and they cause a nasty sting!

THAT SMARTS!

The name "urchin" comes from an old word for hedgehog. Sea urchins and hedgehogs both have spiky outsides.

Most sea urchins grow to be 2 to 4 inches (5 to 10 cm) across.

Urchins Found

Sea urchins have been around for about 450 million years! They can be found living in oceans all over the world, including off the coast of both Maine and California, and around the islands of Hawaii.

While some types of sea urchin are found in colder waters, most like waters that are more **tropical**. They like areas close to shore that have rocky bottoms and other places they can **anchor** themselves. Sea urchins are commonly found around **coral reefs**, too.

That Smarts!

Sea urchins and sea stars belong to the same family of sea creatures. Both have spiny features and are made of five segments, or parts. Neither has a head!

Black sea urchins are common in tropical places.

Body Talk

A sea urchin has a **skeleton**, called a test, made up of several bony plates. Its spines are connected to some of these plates. Other plates have tiny holes in them. Little tubes with a sucker cup on the end come out of the holes. These "tube feet" help the sea urchin move.

Sea urchins have a mouth with five teeth on their underside. They eat mainly **algae** and small pieces of other creatures' leftovers. Their tube feet help bring food to their mouth.

THAT SMARTS!

*Sea urchins are **sensitive** to touch. If poked, a sea urchin can move its sharp spines toward the touch to protect itself.*

The length and sharpness of sea urchin spines differ between species, or kinds, of the animal. Some species don't have spines at all!

Hanging Around

A sea urchin is always looking for food. It spends daylight hours anchored to a hard surface or hiding in a crack or hole for protection. At night, it will slowly move over coral reefs, rocks, and the seafloor looking for food. When food is found, it will use its teeth to scrape it off.

A sea urchin has no eyes. How can it tell the difference between night and day? Scientists report that sea urchins' tube feet can sense light!

THAT SMARTS!

Most sea urchins live to be 20 to 30 years old, but red sea urchins are thought to live up to 200 years.

Sea urchins use their tube feet, teeth, and spines to work their way into holes and cracks during the day.

Ouch!

Sea urchins are sensitive to possible danger, but **passive**. The most common way animals and people get hurt is by simply touching one! A sharp spine could pierce your skin and break off, causing a deep cut. The spine may have venom inside, which can make the wound even more painful.

What's worse is a sting from the small pedicellariae found between the sea urchin's spines. These are somewhat like tiny **jaws** that can grab onto things. They're venomous, too!

That Smarts!

It's common for a victim to have several stings from one sea urchin.

Pedicellariae help a sea urchin grab things floating between its spines as well as protect it from predators.

Watch Your Step

Carelessness causes most sea urchin stings. People walking through shallow water can step on them. Others try to pick up a sea urchin and don't know how to do so safely. Divers and **snorkelers** near sea urchins can get hurt because the spines break off easily.

However, like sea stars, some sea urchins can regrow their body parts! So, if they lose a spine to a careless swimmer, a new one might be able to take its place.

THAT SMARTS!

Sea urchins come in many different colors, including black, brown, green, red, white, and purple.

If you're stung by a sea urchin, take out any spines and scrape away any pedicellariae. Hold the wound in hot water for 30 to 90 minutes. Then clean it with warm water and soap.

Part of the Web

Sea urchins play an important role in the ocean. They keep the amount of algae in check. In fact, when pollution off the coast of Jamaica caused the death of large numbers of urchins, the coral became so overrun with algae that it died!

Too many sea urchins can cause harm, too. They eat up algae needed by other creatures on a coral reef. To keep the balance, sea urchins are food for many kinds of fish, otters, seabirds, sea stars, and crabs.

THAT SMARTS!

Triggerfish blow a jet of water at a sea urchin to flip it over. They avoid the short spines on the underside and peck at the shell to get their dinner.

An eel tries its luck nibbling at a sea urchin.

Sea Urchin for Lunch?

People all over the world eat raw, or uncooked, creatures from the sea. Raw fish, oysters, squid, and octopus are just some of those that are commonly eaten. Sea urchins aren't just eaten raw, though. They're often eaten while still alive!

When served a sea urchin, people flip it over and use a sharp knife to open it up, taking care around the spines. Then, they take out the meat inside and go for it! People say that they have a sweet and earthy flavor.

That Smarts!

Some people open up sea urchins and eat them right on the beach.

People don't need to worry about sea urchin venom once the sea urchin is opened up to be eaten. This image clearly shows the five soft body parts of a sea urchin that can be eaten.

Amazing Urchins

In addition to their stinging, stabbing body parts, sea urchins have another way to protect themselves. They hide by covering their body with small rocks!

Sea urchins need some protection from people, too. When in the ocean, keep watch of where you're walking. Stepping on a sea urchin will hurt both you and the little creature! Trying to reduce pollution protects the amazing sea urchin, as well. Overfishing for food can also harm their populations. We don't want to lose this cool animal!

THAT SMARTS!

If water is polluted, many sea urchins will begin to lose their spines.

Sea urchins are considered threatened species in some places. That means their populations are too low.

Glossary

algae: plantlike living things that are mostly found in water

anchor: to fix or secure

coral reef: an underwater hill made up of the hard parts of tiny sea animals

jaws: the walls of the mouth

passive: not active

pierce: to make a hole through

protect: to keep safe

sensitive: easily affected or annoyed

skeleton: the bony frame of the body

snorkeler: someone who is swimming facedown near the surface of the water while using a tube called a snorkel to breathe

spine: one of many stiff, pointed parts growing from an animal

tropical: having to do with the warm parts of Earth near the equator

venomous: able to produce a liquid called venom that is harmful to other animals

For More Information

Books

Magby, Meryl. *Sea Urchins.* New York, NY: PowerKids Press, 2013.

West, David. *Tide Pool Animals.* Mankato, MN: Smart Apple Media, 2014.

Websites

Sea Urchin
a-z-animals.com/animals/sea-urchin/
Learn even more about sea urchins.

Sea Urchin Facts
www.softschools.com/facts/animals/sea_urchin_facts/479/
This link has lots of fun facts about sea urchins.

Publisher's note to educators and parents: Our editors have carefully reviewed these websites to ensure that they are suitable for students. Many websites change frequently, however, and we cannot guarantee that a site's future contents will continue to meet our high standards of quality and educational value. Be advised that students should be closely supervised whenever they access the Internet.

Index

algae 8, 16

body 4, 14, 19, 20

colors 14

coral reefs 6, 10, 16

food 8, 10, 16, 20

mouth 8

pedicellariae 4, 12, 13, 15

people 4, 12, 14, 18, 19, 20

pollution 16, 20

protection 4, 10, 13, 20

rocks 6, 10, 20

skeleton 8

species 9, 21

spines 4, 6, 8, 9, 11, 12, 13, 14, 15, 16, 18, 20

sting treatment 15

teeth 8, 10, 11

test 8

tropical waters 6, 7

tube feet 8, 10, 11

venom 4, 12, 19